First Three Wagon Trains

Binford & Mort Publishing's hundred page, illustrated, large type
FAR WESTERN CLASSICS editied by Alfred Powers

No. 1. First Three Wagon Trains
No. 2. Adventures on the Columbia River

First Three Wagon Trains

To California, 1841
To Oregon, 1842
To Washington, 1853

By

JOHN BIDWELL
HUBERT HOWE BANCROFT
JAMES LONGMIRE

Pictures by

Frederic Remington and others

FOUNDED · 1891

Binford & Mort Publishing
Portland, Oregon

First Three Wagon Trains

Printed in the United States of America

ISBN: 0-8323-0504-9 (softcover)

First Printing 1956
Second Printing 1993

EARLIEST SETTLER CARAVANS

Previously there had been explorers and trappers all up and down the western trails. A few of the missionaries had come overland. And some small groups of settlers had crossed the plains, notably the Peoria Party in 1839.

But the three wagon trains in these vivid narratives were the real first in each instance to the three states forming the Pacific side of the nation. They had a commonwealth as well as the sunset in their eyes.

The Bidwell americanos *worried the Mexican government; the Elijah White immigrants worried the Hudson's Bay Company; the Naches Pass arrivals worried the Indians— premonitory of the three dispossessions.*

The only whole-distance wagons were by the terriblest route of all, over the roadless Cascades to Puget Sound. The Bidwell party abandoned their wagons on the Salt Desert; five years later these were used by another party as firewood for cooking their suppers. The Elijah White company left some wagons at Fort Laramie, some at Green River, and all the rest at Fort Hall.

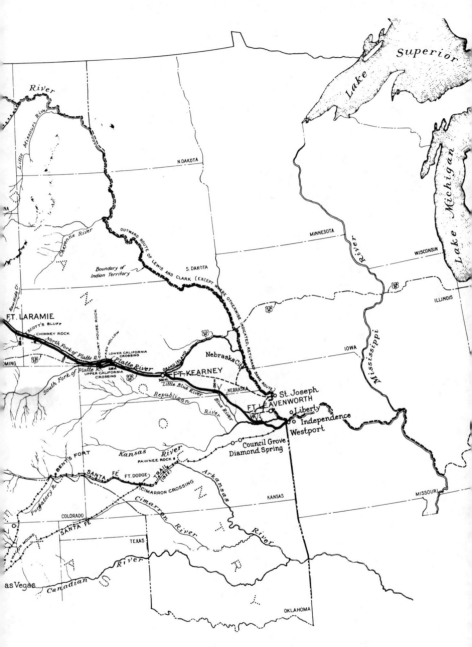

OREGON TRAIL
AS OF 1846
COMPILED FROM AUTHENTIC DATA

United States Department of Agriculture
Bureau of Public Roads
WASHINGTON, D.C.

MAY 15, 1938   DRAWN BY L.E. KNIGHT

1

FIRST EMIGRANT TRAIN TO CALIFORNIA

Kansas River to Marsh's Rancho
May 19 to November 5, 1841

Over a period of forty-seven years John Bidwell wrote three accounts of the emigration of 1841 across the Salt Desert and through the Sierras.

The first, A Journey to California, *a pamphlet of 32 pages—with no date or place on the title page but probably printed at Independence, Missouri, in 1842 —had become so scarce by 1921 that the Bancroft Library copy was the only one known at that time.*

The second was a manuscript of 233 folio pages in longhand dictated in 1877 by Bidwell to a Bancroft assistant. There was much in it besides recollections of the journey but contained, said Bancroft, "a very good narrative of the trip."

The third, which is the one reprinted in this volume, was published in the Century Magazine for November, 1890. Though originally issued in the tens of thousands, it is, after sixty-six years, also scarce and hard to come by.

Four other members of the Bidwell party chronicled the trip in some detail, and several more gave short newspaper descriptions.

Of the company as far as Bear River, two reverend gentlemen, Father DeSmet and Preacher Williams, gave their remembrances in a book apiece. The latter repeatedly lamented the profanity and general ungodliness of the California outfit.

Bidwell became very prominent and a great landholder. In 1892, two years after the Century ran his narrative, he was prohibition candidate for President.

Bidwell-Bartleson Journey

By John Bidwell

In the spring of 1839—living at the time in the western part of Ohio—being then in my twentieth year, I conceived a desire to see the great prairies of the West, especially those most frequently spoken of, in Illinois, Iowa, and Missouri. Emigration from the East was tending westward, and settlers had already begun to invade those rich fields.

Starting on foot to Cincinnati, ninety miles distant, I fortunately got a chance to ride most of the way on a wagon loaded with farm produce. My outfit consisted of about $75, the clothes I wore, and a few others in a knapsack which I carried in the usual way strapped upon my shoulders, for in those days travelers did not have valises or trunks. Though traveling was considered dangerous, I had no weapon more formidable than a pocket-knife. From Cincinnati I went down the Ohio River by steamboat to the Mississippi, up the Mississippi to St. Louis, and thence to Burlington, in what was then the Territory of Iowa.

Those were bustling days on the western rivers, which were then the chief highways of travel. The scenes at the wood landings I recall as particularly lively and picturesque. Many passengers would save a little by helping to "wood the boat," *i. e.*, by carrying wood down the bank and throwing it on the boat, a special ticket being issued on that condition. It was very interesting to see the long lines of passengers coming up the gang-plank, each with two or three sticks of wood on his shoulders.

An anecdote is told of an Irishman who boarded a western steamer and wanted to know the fare to St. Louis, and, being told, asked, "What do you charge for 150 pounds of freight?" Upon learning the price, a small amount, he announced that he would go as freight.

"All right," said the captain, "put him down in the hold and lay some flour barrels on him to keep him down."

In 1839 Burlington had perhaps not over two hundred inhabitants, though it was the capital of Iowa Territory.

After working awhile at putting up a log house—until all the people in the neighborhood became ill with fever and ague—I concluded to move on and strike out to the south and southwest into Missouri.

On the route I traveled I cannot recall seeing an emigrant wagon in Missouri. The western movement, which subsequently filled Missouri and other Western States and overflowed into the adjoining Territory, had then hardly begun.

On my arrival, my money being all spent, I was obliged to accept the first thing that was offered, and began teaching school in the country about five miles from the town of Weston, which was located on the north side of the Missouri River and about four miles from Fort Leavenworth in Kansas Territory.

I taught school there in all about a year. My arrival was in June, 1839, and in the fall of that year the surveyors came on to lay out the country: the lines ran every way, sometimes through a man's house, sometimes through his barn, so that there was much confusion and trouble about boundaries. By the favor of certain men, and by paying a small amount for a little piece of fence here and a small clearing there, I got a claim, and purposed to make it my home, and to have my father remove there from Ohio.

In the following summer, 1840, the weather was very hot, so that during the vacation I could do but little work on my place, and needing some supplies,—books, clothes, etc.— I concluded to take a trip to St. Louis, which I did by way of the Missouri River. The distance was six hundred miles by water; the down trip occupied two days, and was one of the most delightful experiences of my life. But returning, the river being low and full of snags, and the steamboat heavily laden,—the boats were generally light going down,—we were continually getting on sand bars, and were delayed nearly a month.

This trip proved to be the turning point in my life, for while I was gone a man had jumped my land. Generally in such cases public sentiment was against the jumper, and it was decidedly so in my case. But the scoundrel held on. He was a bully—had killed a man in Callaway County—and everybody seemed afraid of him. Influential friends of mine tried to persuade him to let me have eighty acres, half of the claim. But he was stubborn, and said that all he wanted was just what the law allowed him. Unfortunately for me, he had the legal advantage. I had worked some now and then on the place, but had not actually lived on it. The law required a certain residence, and that the preemptor should be twenty-one years of age or a man of family. I was neither, and could do nothing. Nearly all I had earned had been spent upon the land, and when that was taken I lost about everything I had. There being no possibility of getting another claim to suit me, I resolved to go elsewhere when spring should open.

In November or December of 1840, while still teaching school in Platte County, I came across a Frenchman named Roubideaux, who said he had been to California. He had been a trader in New Mexico, and had followed the road traveled by traders from the frontier of Missouri to Santa Fe. He had probably gone through what is now New Mexico and Arizona into California by the Gila River trail used by the Mexicans. His description of California was in the superlative degree favorable, so much so that I resolved if possible to see that wonderful land, and with others helped to get up a meeting at Weston and invited him to make a statement before it in regard to the country. At that time when a man moved out West, as soon as he was fairly settled he wanted to move again, and naturally every question imaginable was asked in regard to this wonderful country. Roubideaux described it as one of perennial spring and boundless fertility, and laid stress on the countless thousands of wild horses and cattle. He told about oranges, and hence must have been at Los Angeles, or the mission of San Gabriel, a few miles from it.

Every conceivable question that we could

ask him was answered favorably. Generally the first question which a Missourian asked about a country was whether there was any fever and ague. I remember his answer distinctly. He said there was but one man in California that had ever had a chill there, and it was a matter of so much wonderment to the people of Monterey that they went eighteen miles into the country to see him shake. Nothing could have been more satisfactory on the score of health.

He said that the Spanish authorities were most friendly, and that the people were the most hospitable on the globe; that you could travel all over California and it would cost you nothing for horses or food. Even the Indians were friendly. His description of the country made it seem like a Paradise.

The result was that we appointed a corresponding secretary, and a committee to report a plan of organization. A pledge was drawn up in which every signer agreed to purchase a suitable outfit, and to rendezvous at Sapling Grove in what is now the State of Kansas, on the 9th of the following May, armed and equipped to cross the Rocky Mountains to California. We called ourselves the Western Emigration Society, and as soon as the pledge was drawn up every one who agreed to come signed his name to it, and it took like wildfire.

In a short time, I think within a month, we had about five hundred names; we also had correspondence on the subject with people all over Missouri, and even as far east as Illinois and Kentucky, and as far south as Arkansas. As soon as the movement was announced in the papers we had many letters of inquiry, and we expected people in considerable numbers to join us. About that time we heard of a man living in Jackson County, Missouri, who had received a letter from a person in California named Dr. Marsh, speaking favorably of the country, and a copy of this letter was published.

Our ignorance of the route was complete. We knew that California lay west, and that was the extent of our knowledge. Some of the maps consulted, supposed of course to be correct, showed a lake in the vicinity of where Salt Lake now is; it was represented as a long lake, three or four hundred miles in extent, narrow and with two outlets, both running into the Pacific Ocean, either apparently larger than the Mississippi River. An intelligent man with whom I boarded—Elam Brown, who till recently lived in California, dying when over ninety years of age—possessed a map that showed these rivers to be large, and he advised me to take tools along to make canoes, so that if we found the country so rough that we could not get along with our wagons we could descend one of those rivers to the Pacific. Even Frémont knew nothing about Salt Lake until 1843, when for the first time he explored it and mapped it correctly, his report being first printed, I think, in 1845.

This being the first movement to cross the Rocky Mountains to California, it is not surprising that it suffered reverses before we were fairly started. One of these was the publication of a letter in a New York newspaper giving a depressing view of the country for which we were all so confidently longing. It seems that in 1837 or 1838 a man by the name of Farnham, a lawyer, went from New York City into the Rocky Mountains for his health. He was an invalid, hopelessly gone with consumption it was thought, and as a last resort he went into the mountains, traveled with the trappers, lived in the open air as the trappers lived, eating only meat as they did, and in two or three years he entirely regained his health; but instead of returning east by way of St. Louis, as he had gone, he went down the Columbia River and took a vessel to Monterey and thence to San Blas, making his way through Mexico to New York. Upon his return—in February or March, 1841—he published the letter mentioned. His bad opinion of California was based wholly on his unfortunate experience in Monterey, which I will recount.

In 1840 there lived in California an old Rocky Mountaineer by the name of Isaac Graham. He was injudicious in his talk, and by boasting that the United States or Texas would some day take California, he excited the hostility and jealousy of the people. In those days Americans were held in disfavor by the native Californians on account of the war made by Americans in Texas to wrest Texas from Mexico. The number of Americans in California at this time was very small. When I went to California in 1841 all the foreigners—and all were foreigners except Indians and Mexicans—did not, I think, exceed one hundred; nor was the character of all of them the most prepossessing.

Some had been trappers in the Rocky Mountains who had not seen civilization for a quarter of a century; others were men who had found their way to California, as Roubideaux had done, by way of Mexico; others still had gone down the Columbia River to Oregon and joined trapping parties in the service of the Hudson Bay Company going from Oregon to California—men who would let their beards grow down to their knees, and wear buckskin garments made and fringed like those of the Indians, and who considered it a compliment to be told, "I took ye for an Injin." Another class of men from the Rocky Mountains were in the habit of making their way by the Mohave Desert south of the Sierra Nevada into California to steal horses, sometimes driving off four or five hundred at a time. The other Americans, most numerous perhaps, were sailors who had run away from vessels and remained in the country. With few exceptions this was the character of the American population when I came to California, and they were not generally a class calculated to gain much favor with the people.

Farnham happened to come into the bay of Monterey when this fellow Graham and his confederates, and all others whom the Californians suspected, were under arrest in irons on board a vessel, ready for transportation to San Blas in Mexico, whither indeed they were taken, and where some of them died in irons. I am not sure that at this time the English had a consul in California; but the United States had none, and there was no one there to take the part of the Americans. Farnham, being a lawyer, doubtless knew that the proceeding was illegal. He went ashore and protested against it, but without effect, as he was only a private individual. Probably he was there on a burning hot day, and saw only the dreary sandhills to the east of the old town of Monterey. On arriving in New York he published the letter referred to, describing how Americans were oppressed by the native Californians, and how dangerous it was for Americans to go there.

2

The merchants of Platte County had all along protested against our going and had tried from the beginning to discourage and break up the movement, saying it was the most unheard-of, foolish, wild-goose chase that ever entered into the brain of man for five hundred people to pull up stakes, leave that beautiful country, and go away out to a region that we knew nothing of. But they made little headway until this letter of Farnham's appeared. They republished it in a paper in the town of Liberty in Clay County —there being no paper published in Platte County—and sent it broadcast all over the surrounding region.

The result was that as the people began to think more seriously about the scheme the membership of the society began dropping off, and so it happened at last that of all the five hundred that signed the pledge I was the only one that got ready; and even I had hard work to do so, for I had barely means to buy a wagon, a gun, and provisions. Indeed, the man who was going with me, and who was to furnish the horses, backed out, and there I was with my wagon!

During the winter, to keep the project alive, I had made two or three trips into Jackson County, Missouri, crossing the Missouri River, always dangerous in winter when ice was running, by the ferry at Westport Landing, now Kansas City. Sometimes I had to go ten miles farther down—sixty miles from Weston—to a safer ferry at Independence Landing in order to get into Jackson County, to see men who were talking of going to California, and to get information.

At the last moment before the time to start for the rendezvous at Sapling Grove—it seemed almost providential—along came a man named George Henshaw, an invalid, from Illinois, I think. He was pretty well dressed, was riding a fine black horse, and had ten or fifteen dollars. I persuaded him to let me take his horse and trade him for a yoke of steers to pull the wagon and a sorry-looking, one-eyed mule for him to ride. We went *via* Weston to lay in some supplies. One wagon and four or five persons here joined us.

On leaving Weston, where there had been so much opposition, we were six or seven in number, and nearly half the town followed us for a mile, and some for five or six miles, to bid us good-by, showing the deep interest felt in our journey. All expressed good wishes and desired to hear from us.

3

When we reached Sapling Grove, the place of rendezvous, in May, 1841, there was but one wagon ahead of us. For the next few days one or two wagons would come each day, and among the recruits were three families from Arkansas. We organized by electing as captain of the company a man named Bartleson from Jackson County, Missouri. He was not the best man for the position, but we were given to understand that if he was not elected captain he would not go; and as he had seven or eight men with him, and we did not want the party diminished, he was chosen.

Every one furnished his own supplies. The party consisted of sixty-nine, including men, women, and children. Our teams were of oxen, mules, and horses. We had no cows, as the later emigrants usually had, and the lack of milk was a great deprivation to the children. It was understood that every one should have not less than a barrel of flour with sugar and so forth to suit; but I laid in one hundred pounds of flour more than the usual quantity, besides other things. This I did because we were told that when we got into the mountains we probably would get out of bread and have to live on meat alone, which I thought would kill me even if it did not others.

My gun was an old flint-lock rifle, but a good one. Old hunters told me to have nothing to do with cap or percussion locks, that they were unreliable, and that if I got my caps or percussion wet I could not shoot, while if I lost my flint I could pick up another on the plains.

I doubt whether there was one hundred dollars in money in the whole party, but all were enthusiastic and anxious to go.

In five days after my arrival we were ready to start, but no one knew where to go, not even the captain. Finally a man came up, one of the last to arrive, and announced that a company of Catholic missionaries were on their way from St. Louis to the Flathead nation of Indians with an old Rocky Mountaineer for a guide, and that if we would wait another day they would be up with us. At first we were independent, and thought we could not afford to wait for a slow missionary party. But when we found that no one knew which way to go, we sobered down and waited for them to come up; and it was well we did, for otherwise probably not one of us would ever have reached California, because of our inexperience. Afterwards when we came in contact with Indians our people were so easily excited that if we had not had with us an old mountaineer the result would certainly have been disastrous.

The name of the guide was Captain Fitzpatrick; he had been at the head of trapping parties in the Rocky Mountains for many years. He and the missionary party went with us as far as Soda Springs, now in Idaho Territory, whence they turned north to the Flathead nation. The party consisted of three Roman Catholic priests—Father De Smet, Father Pont, Father Mengarini—and ten or eleven French Canadians, and accompanying them were an old mountaineer named John Gray and a young Englishman named Romaine, and also a man named Baker. They seemed glad to have us with them, and we certainly were glad to have their company.

Father De Smet had been to the Flathead

nation before. He had gone out with a trapping party, and on his return had traveled with only a guide by another route, farther to the north and through hostile tribes. He was genial, of fine presence, and one of the saintliest men I have ever known, and I cannot wonder that the Indians were made to believe him divinely protected. He was a man of great kindness and great affability under all circumstances; nothing seemed to disturb his temper. The Canadians had mules and Red River carts, instead of wagons and horses, —two mules to each cart, five or six of them, —and in case of steep hills they would hitch three or four of the animals to one cart, always working them tandem. Sometimes a cart would go over, breaking everything in it to pieces; and at such times Father De Smet would be just the same—beaming with good humor.

4

In general our route lay from near Westport, where Kansas City now is, northwesterly over the prairie, crossing several streams, till we struck the Platte River. Then we followed along the south side of the Platte to and a day's journey or so along the South Fork. Here the features of the country became more bold and interesting.

Then crossing the South Fork of the Platte, and following up the north side for a day or so, we went over to the North Fork and camped at Ash Hollow; thence up the north side of that fork, passing those noted landmarks known as the Court House Rocks, Chimney Rock, Scott's Bluffs, till we came to Fort Laramie, a trading post of the American Fur Company, near which was Lupton's Fort, belonging, as I understood, to some rival company.

Thence after several days we came to another noted landmark called Independence Rock, on a branch of the North Platte called the Sweetwater, which we followed up to the head, soon after striking the Little Sandy, and then the Big Sandy, which empties into Green River.

Next we crossed Green River to Black Fork, which we followed up till we came to Ham's Fork, at the head of which we crossed the divide between Green and Bear rivers. Then we followed Bear River down to Soda Springs.

The waters of Bear Lake discharged through that river, which we continued to follow down on the west side till we came to Salt Lake. Then we went around the north end of the lake and struck out to the west and southwest.

For a time, until we reached the Platte River, one day was much like another. We set forth every morning and camped every night, detailing men to stand guard. Captain Fitzpatrick and the missionary party would generally take the lead and we would follow. Fitzpatrick knew all about the Indian tribes, and when there was any danger we kept in a more compact body, to protect one another. At other times we would be scattered along, sometimes for half a mile or more. We were generally together, because there was often work to be done to avoid delay. We had to make the road, frequently digging down steep banks, filling gulches, removing stones. In such cases everybody would take a spade or do something to help make the road passable.

When we camped at night we usually drew the wagons and carts together in a hollow square and picketed our animals inside in the corral. The wagons were common ones and of no special pattern, and some of them were covered. The tongue of one would be fastened to the back of another. To lessen the danger from Indians, we usually had no fires at night and did our cooking in the daytime.

The first incident was a scare that we had

from a party of Cheyenne Indians just before we reached the Platte River, about two weeks after we set out. One of our men who chanced to be out hunting, some distance from the company and behind us, suddenly appeared without mule, gun, or pistol, and lacking most of his clothes, and in great excitement reported that he had been surrounded by thousands of Indians.

The company, too, became excited, and Captain Fitzpatrick tried, but with little effect, to control and pacify them. Every man started his team into a run, till the oxen, like the mules and horses, were in a full gallop. Captain Fitzpatrick went ahead and directed them to follow, and as fast as they came to the bank of the river he put the wagons in the form of a hollow square and had all the animals securely picketed within.

After a while the Indians came in sight. There were only forty of them, but they were well mounted on horses, and were evidently a war party, for they had no women except one, a medicine woman. They came up and camped within a hundred yards of us on the river below. Fitzpatrick told us that they would not have come in that way if they were hostile.

Our hunter in his excitement said that there

were thousands of them, and that they had robbed him of his gun, mule, and pistol. When the Indians had put up their lodges Fitzpatrick and John Gray, the old hunter mentioned, went out to them and by signs were made to understand that the Indians did not intend to hurt the man or to take his mule or gun, but that he was so excited when he saw them that they had to disarm him to keep him from shooting them; they did not know what had become of his pistol or of his clothes, which he said they had torn off. They surrendered the mule and the gun, thus showing that they were friendly. They proved to be Cheyenne Indians. Ever afterwards that man went by the name of Cheyenne Dawson.

As soon as we struck the buffalo country we found a new source of interest. Before reaching the Platte we had seen an abundance of antelope and elk, prairie wolves and villages of prairie dogs, but only an occasional buffalo. We now began to kill buffaloes for food, and at the suggestion of John Gray, and following the practice of Rocky Mountain white hunters, our people began to kill them just to get the tongues and the marrow bones, leaving all the rest of the meat on the plains for the wolves to eat. But the Cheyennes, who traveled ahead of us for two or three days, set us a better example. At their camps we noticed that when they killed buffaloes they took all the meat, everything but the bones. Indians were never wasteful of the buffalo except in winter for the sake of the robes, and then only in order to get the whisky which traders offered them in exchange.

There is no better beef in the world than that of the buffalo; it is also very good jerked, *i. e.,* cut into strings and thoroughly dried. It was an easy matter to kill buffaloes after we got to where they were numerous, by keeping out of sight and to the leeward of them. I think I can truly say that I saw in that region in one day more buffaloes than I have seen of cattle in all my life. I have seen the plain black with them for several days' journey as far as the eye could reach. They seemed to be coming northward continually from the distant plains to the Platte to get water, and would plunge in and swim across by thousands—so numerous were they that they changed not only the color of the water, but its taste, until it was unfit to drink; but we had to use it.

One night when we were encamped on the South Fork of the Platte they came in such droves that we had to sit up and fire guns and make what fires we could to keep them from running over us and trampling us into the dust. We were obliged to go out some distance from camp to turn them: Captain Fitzpatrick told us that if we did not do this the buffaloes in front could not turn aside for the pressure of those behind. We could hear them thundering all night long; the ground fairly trembled with vast approaching bands; and if they had not been diverted, wagons, animals, and emigrants would have been trodden under their feet.

One cannot nowadays describe the rush and wildness of the thing. A strange feature was that when old oxen, tired and foot-sore, got among a buffalo herd, as they sometimes would in the night, they would soon become as wild as the wildest buffalo; and if ever recovered it was because they could not run so fast as the buffaloes or one's horse. The ground over which the herds trampled was left rather barren, but buffalo-grass being short and curling, in traveling over it they did not cut it up as much as they would other kinds.

On the Platte River, on the afternoon of one of the hottest days we experienced on the plains, we had a taste of a cyclone: first came a terrific shower, followed by a fall of hail to the depth of four inches, some of the stones being as large as turkeys' eggs; and the next day a waterspout—an angry, huge, whirling cloud column, which seemed to draw its water from the Platte River—passed within a quarter of a mile behind us. We stopped and braced ourselves against our wagons to keep them from being overturned. Had it struck us it doubtless would have demolished us.

Above the junction of the forks of the Platte we continued to pass notable natural formations—first O'Fallon's Bluffs, then Court House Rocks, a group of fantastic shapes to which some of our party started to go. After they had gone what seemed fifteen or twenty miles the huge pile looked just as far off as when they started, and so they turned and came back—so deceptive are distances in the clear atmosphere of the Rocky Mountains.

A noted landmark on the North Fork, which we sighted fifty miles away, was Chimney Rock. It was then nearly square, and I think it must have been fifty feet higher than now, though after we passed it a portion of it fell off.

Scott's Bluffs are known to emigrants for their picturesqueness. These formations, like those first mentioned, are composed of indurated yellow clay or soft sand rock; they are washed and broken into all sorts of fantastic forms by the rains and storms of ages, and have the appearance of an immense city of towers and castles. They are quite difficult to explore, as I learned by experience in an effort to pursue and kill mountain sheep or big-horn. These were seen in great numbers, but we failed to kill any, as they inhabit places almost inaccessible and are exceedingly wild.

As we ascended the Platte buffaloes became scarcer, and on the Sweetwater none were to be seen. Now appeared in the distance to the north of west, gleaming under its mantle of perpetual snow, that lofty range known as the Wind River Mountains. It was the first time I had seen snow in summer; some of the peaks were very precipitous, and the view was alto-gether most impressive.

Guided by Fitzpatrick, we crossed the Rockies at or near the South Pass, where the mountains were apparently low. Some years before a man named William Sublette, an Indian fur trader, went to the Rocky Moun-tains with goods in wagons, and those were the only wagons that had ever been there be-fore us; sometimes we came across the tracks, but generally they were obliterated, and thus were of no service.

Approaching Green River in the Rocky Mountains, it was found that some of the wagons, including Captain Bartleson's, had alcohol on board, and that the owners wanted to find trappers in the Rocky Mountains to

Westport Landing, later Kansas City, where Bidwell talked up the trip to California.

FREDERIC REMINGTON—

Nearing the Platte, led by Captain Fitzpatrick, famous Mountain Man.

A halt on the plains for a powwow with a band of Cheyennes.

Splitting the buffalo herd. "Our people began to kill them just to get the tongues and the marrow bones."

whom they might sell it. This was a surprise to many of us, as there had been no drinking on the way. John Gray was sent ahead to see if he could find a trapping party, and he was instructed, if successful, to have them come to a certain place on Green River. He struck a trail, and overtook a party on their way to the buffalo region to lay in provisions, *i. e.,* buffalo meat, and they returned, and came and camped on Green River very soon after our arrival, buying the greater part, if not all, of the alcohol, it first having been diluted so as to make what they called whisky—three or four gallons of water to a gallon of alcohol. Years afterwards we heard of the fate of that party: they were attacked by Indians the very first night after they left us and several of them killed, including the captain of the trapping party, whose name was Frapp. The whisky was probably the cause.

Several years ago when I was going down Weber Canyon, approaching Salt Lake, swiftly borne along on an observation car amid cliffs and over rushing streams, something said that night at the campfire on Green River was forcibly recalled to mind. We had in our party an illiterate fellow named Bill Overton, who in the evening at one of the campfires loudly declared that nothing in his life had ever surprised him. Of course that raised a dispute.

"Never surprised in your life?"

"No, I never was surprised." And, more-over, he swore that nothing ever *could* surprise him. "I should not be surprised," said he, "if I were to see a steamboat come plowing over these mountains this minute." In rattling down the canyon of Weber River it occurred to me that the reality was almost equal to Bill Overton's extravaganza, and I could but won-der what he would have said had he suddenly come upon this modern scene.

5

As I have said, at Soda Springs—at the northernmost bend of Bear River—our party separated. It was a bright and lovely place. The abundance of soda water, including the intermittent gushing so-called Steamboat Spring; the beautiful fir and cedar covered hills; the huge piles of red or brown sinter, the result of fountains once active but then dry—all these, together with the river, lent a charm to its wild beauty and made the spot a notable one. Here the missionary party were to turn north and go into the Flathead nation. Fort Hall, about forty miles distant on Snake River, lay on their route. There was no road; but something like a trail, doubtless used by the trappers, led in that direction. From Fort Hall there was also a trail down Snake River, by which trapping parties reached the Columbia River and Fort Vancouver, the headquarters of the Hudson Bay Company.

Our party, originally sixty-nine, including women and children, had become lessened to sixty-four in number. One had accidentally shot and killed himself at the forks of the Platte. Another of our party, named Simpson, had left us at Fort Laramie. Three had turned back from Green River, intending to make their way to Fort Bridger and await an opportunity to return home. Their names were Peyton, Rodgers, and Amos E. Frye. Thirty-two of our party, becoming discouraged, decided not to venture without path or guide into the unknown and trackless region towards California, but concluded to go with the missionary party to Fort Hall and thence find their way down Snake and Columbia rivers into Oregon.[1]

The rest of us—also thirty-two in number,

1 Of the party leaving us at Soda Springs to go into Oregon I can now, after the lapse of forty-nine years, recall by their names only the following: Mr. Williams and wife; Samuel Kelsey, his wife and five children; Joshiah Kelsey and wife; C. W. Flugge; Mr. Carroll; Mr. Fowler; a Methodist Episcopal preacher, whose name I think was also Williams; "Cheyenne Dawson"; and another called "Bear Dawson." Subsequently we heard that the party safely arrived in Oregon, and some of them we saw in California. One (C. W. Flugge) was in time to join a party and come from Oregon to California in the same year (1841).

including Benjamin Kelsey, his wife and little daughter—remained firm, refusing to be diverted from our original purpose of going direct to California. After getting all the information we could from Captain Fitzpatrick, we regretfully bade good-by to our fellow emigrants and to Father De Smet and his party.

We were now thrown entirely upon our own resources. All the country beyond was to us a veritable *terra incognita,* and we only knew that California lay to the west. Captain Fitzpatrick was not much better informed, but he had heard that parties had penetrated the country to the southwest and west of Salt Lake to trap for beaver; and by his advice four of our men went with the parties to Fort Hall to consult Captain Grant, who was in charge there, and to gain information. Meanwhile our depleted party slowly made its way down the west side of Bear River.

Our separation at Soda Springs recalls an incident. The days were usually very hot, the nights almost freezing. The first day our little company went only about ten miles and camped on Bear River. In company with a man named James John—always called "Jimmy John"—I wandered a mile or two down the river fishing.

Seeing snow on a high mountain to the

west we longed to reach it, for the heat where we were was intense. So, without losing time to get our guns or coats or to give notice at the camp, we started direct for the snow, with the impression that we could go and return by sundown. But there intervened a range of lower mountains, a certain peak of which seemed almost to touch the snow. Both of us were fleet of foot and made haste, but we only gained the summit of the peak about sundown. The distance must have been twelve or fifteen miles. A valley intervened, and the snow lay on a higher mountain beyond.

I proposed to camp. But Jimmy gave me a disdainful look, as much as to say, "You are afraid to go," and quickened his gait into a run down the mountain towards the snow. I called to him to stop, but he would not even look back.

A firm resolve seized me—to overtake him, but not again to ask him to return. We crossed the valley in the night, saw many Indian camp-fires, and gained a sharp ridge leading up to the snow. This was first brushy and then rough and rocky. The brush had no paths except those made by wild animals; the rocks were sharp, and soon cut through our moccasins and made our feet bleed. But up and up we went until long after midnight, and until a cloud covered the mountain. We were above timberline, excepting a few stunted fir trees, under one of which we crawled to wait for day, for it was too dark to see.

Day soon dawned, but we were almost frozen. Our fir tree nest had been the lair of grizzly bears that had wallowed there and shed quantities of shaggy hair. The snow was still beyond, and we had lost both sight and direction. But in an hour or two we reached it. It was nearly as hard as ice. Filling a large handkerchief, without taking time to admire the scenery we started towards the camp by a new route, for our feet were too sore to go by the rocky ridge by which we had come.

But the new way led to trouble. There were thickets so dense as to exclude the sun, and roaring little streams in deep dark chasms; we had to crawl through paths which looked untrodden except by grizzlies; in one place a large bear had passed evidently only a few minutes before, crossing the deep gorge, plunging through the wild, dashing water, and wetting the steep bank as he went up. We carried our drawn butcher knives in our hands, for they were our only weapons.

At last we emerged into the valley. Apparently numerous Indians had left that very morning, as shown by the tracks of lodge poles drawn on the ground. Making haste, we soon gained the hills, and at about 2 P. M. sighted our wagons, already two or three miles on the march. When our friends saw us they stopped, and all who could ran to welcome us. They had given us up for lost, supposing that we had been killed by the hostile Blackfeet, who, as Captain Fitzpatrick had warned us, sometimes roamed through that region.

The company had barricaded the camp at night as best they could, and every man had spent a sleepless night on guard. Next morning they passed several hours in scouring the country. Their first questions were: "Where have you been?" "Where have you been?"

I was able to answer triumphantly, *"We have been up to the snow!"* and to demonstrate the fact by showing all the snow I had left, which was now reduced to a ball about the size of my fist.

6

In about ten days our four men returned from Fort Hall, during which time we had advanced something over one hundred miles towards Salt Lake. They brought the information that we must strike out west of Salt Lake—as it was even then called by the trappers—being careful not to go too far south, lest we should get into a waterless country without grass. They also said we must be careful not to go too far north, lest we should get into a broken country and steep canyons, and wander about, as trapping parties had been known to do, and become bewildered and perish.

September had come before we reached Salt Lake, which we struck at its northern extremity. Part of the time we had purposely traveled slowly to enable the men from Fort Hall the sooner to overtake us. But unavoidable delays were frequent: daily, often hourly, the road had to be made passable for our wagons by digging down steep banks, filling gulches, etc. Indian fires obscured mountains and valleys in a dense, smoky atmosphere, so that we could not see any considerable distance in order to avoid obstacles.

The principal growth, on plain and hill alike, was the interminable sagebrush (*Artemisia*), and often it was difficult, for miles at a time, to break a road through it, and sometimes a lightly laden wagon would be overturned. Its monotonous dull color and scraggy appearance gave a most dreary aspect to the landscape. But it was not wholly useless: where large enough it made excellent fuel, and it was the home and shelter of the hare—generally known as the "jack rabbit"—and of the sage-hen.

Trees were almost a sure sign of water in that region. But the mirage was most deceptive, magnifying stunted sage-brush on diminutive hillocks into trees and groves.

Thus misled, we traveled all day without water, and at midnight found ourselves in a plain, level as a floor, incrusted with salt, and as white as snow. Crusts of salt broken up by our wagons, and driven by the chilly night wind like ice on the surface of a frozen pond, was to me a most striking counterfeit of a winter scene. This plain became softer and softer until our poor, almost famished, animals could not pull our wagons. In fact, we were going direct to Salt Lake and did not know it.

So, in search of water, we turned from a southerly to an easterly course, and went about ten miles and soon after daylight arrived at Bear River. So near to Salt Lake were we that the water in the river was too salt for us or our animals to use, but we had to use it; it would not quench thirst, but it did save life. The grass looked most luxuriant, and sparkled as if covered with frost. But it was salt; our hungry jaded animals refused to eat it, and we had to lie by a whole day to rest them before we could travel.

Leaving this camp and bearing northwest we crossed our tracks on the salt plain, having thus described a triangle of several miles in dimensions. One of the most serious of our troubles was to find water where we could camp at night. So soon came another hot day, and hard travel all day and all night without water! From a westerly course we turned directly north, and guided by antelope trails, came in a few miles to an abundance of grass and good water. The condition of our animals compelled us to rest here nearly a week. Meanwhile two of the men who had been to Fort Hall went ahead to explore.

Provisions were becoming scarce, and we saw that we must avoid unnecessary delay. The two men were gone about five days. Under their lead we set forth, bearing west, then southwest, around Salt Lake, then again west. After two or three fatiguing days—one day and a night without water—the first notice we had of approach to any considerable mountain was the sight of crags, dimly seen through the smoke, many hundred feet above our heads. Here was plenty of good grass and water.

Nearly all now said, "Let us leave our

wagons, otherwise the snows will overtake us before we get to California." So we stopped one day and threw away everything we could not carry, made pack-saddles and packed the oxen, mules, and horses, and started.

7

On Green River we had seen the style of pack saddles used by the trapping party, and had learned a little about how to make them. Packing is an art, and something that only an experienced mountaineer can do well so as to save his animal and keep his pack from falling off. We were unaccustomed to it, and the difficulties we had at first were simply indescribable. It is much more difficult to fasten a pack on an ox than on a mule or a horse.

The trouble began the very first day. But we started—most of us on foot, for nearly all the animals, including several of the oxen, had to carry packs. It was but a few minutes before the packs began to turn; horses became scared, mules kicked, oxen jumped and bellowed, and articles were scattered in all directions. We took more pains, fixed things, made a new start, and did better, though packs continued occasionally to fall off and delay us.

Those that had better pack-saddles and had tied their loads securely were ahead, while the others were obliged to lag behind, because they had to repack, and sometimes things would be strewn all along the route. The first night I happened to be among those that kept pretty well back, because the horses out-traveled the oxen. The foremost came to a place and stopped where there was no water or grass, and built a fire so that we could see it and come up to them. We got there about midnight, but some of our oxen that had packs had not come up, and among them were my two. So I had to return the next morning and find them, Cheyenne Dawson alone volunteering to go with me.

One man had brought along about a quart of water, which was carefully doled out before we started, each receiving a little canister-cover full—less than half a gill; but as Dawson and I had to go for the oxen, we were given a double portion. This was all the water I had until the next day. It was a burning hot day. We could not find the trail of the oxen for a long time, and Dawson refused to go any farther, saying that there were plenty of cattle in California; but I had to do it, for the oxen were carrying our provisions and other things.

Afterwards I struck the trail, and found that the oxen instead of going west had gone north, and I followed them until nearly sundown. They had got into a grassy country, which showed that they were nearing water. Seeing Indian tracks on their trail following them, I felt there was imminent danger, and at once examined my gun and pistols to see that they were primed and ready. But soon I found my oxen lying down in tall grass by the side of the trail. Seeing no Indians, I hastened to fasten the packs and make my way to overtake the company. They had promised to stop when they came to water and wait for me. I traveled all night, and at early dawn came to where there was plenty of water and where the company had taken their dinner the day before, but they had failed to stop for me according to promise.

I was much perplexed, because I had seen many fires in the night, which I took to be Indian fires, so I fastened my oxen to a scraggy willow and began to make circles around to see which way the company had gone. The ground was so hard that the animals had made no impression, which bewildered me. Finally, while making a circle of about three miles away off to the south, I saw two men coming on horseback. In the glare of the mirage, which distorted everything, I could not tell whether they were Indians or white men, but I supposed them to be Indians, feeling sure our party would go west and not south. In a mirage a man on horseback looks as tall as a tree, and I could only tell by the motion that they were mounted.

I made a beeline to my oxen, to make breast-works of them. In doing this I came to a small stream resembling running water, into which I urged my horse, whereupon he went down into a quagmire, over head and ears, out of sight. My gun also went under the mire. I got hold of something on the bank, threw out my gun, which was full of mud and water, and holding to the rope attached to my horse, by dint of hard pulling I succeeded in getting him out—a sorry sight, his ears and eyes full of mud, and his body covered with it. At last, just in time, I was able to move and get behind the oxen. My gun was in no condition to shoot. However, putting dry powder in the pan I determined to do my best in case the supposed Indians should come up; but lo! they were two of our party coming to meet me, bringing water and provisions. It was a great relief.

I felt indignant that the party had not stopped for me—not the less so when I learned that Captain Bartleson had said, when they started back to find me, that they "would be in better business to go ahead and look for a road." He had not forgotten certain comments of mine on his qualities as a student of Indian character. An instance of this I will relate.

One morning, just as we were packing up, a party of about ninety Indians, on horseback, a regular war party, were descried coming up. Some of us begged the captain to send men out to prevent them from coming to us while we were in the confusion of packing. But he said, "Boys, you must not show any sign of hostility; if you go out there with guns the Indians will think us hostile, and may get mad and hurt us." However, five or six of us took our guns and went out, and by signs made them halt. They did not prove to be hostile, but they had carbines, and if we had been careless and had let them come near they might, and probably would, have killed us. At last we got packed up and started, and the Indians traveled along three or four hundred yards one side or the other of us or behind us all day.

They appeared anxious to trade, and offered a buckskin, well dressed, worth two or three dollars, for three or four charges of powder and three or four balls. This showed that they were in want of ammunition. The carbines indicated that they had had communication with some trading-post belonging to the Hudson's Bay Company. They had buffalo-robes also, which showed that they were a roving hunting party, as there were no buffaloes within three or four hundred miles. At this time I had spoken my mind pretty freely concerning Captain Bartleson's lack of judgment, as one could scarcely help doing under the circumstances.

8

We now got into a country where there was no grass nor water, and then we began to catechize the men who had gone to Fort Hall. They repeated, "If you go too far south you will get into a desert country and your animals will perish; there will be no water nor grass."

We were evidently too far south. We could not go west, and the formation of the country was such that we had to turn and go north across a range of mountains. Having struck a small stream we camped upon it all night, and next day continued down its banks, crossing from side to side, most of the time following Indian paths or paths made by antelope and deer. In the afternoon we entered a canyon the walls of which were precipitous and several hundred feet high. Finally the pleasant bermy banks gave out entirely, and we could travel only in the dry bed of what in the wet season was a raging river. It became a solid mass of stones and huge boulders, and the animals became tender-footed and sore so that they could hardly stand up, and as we continued the way became worse and worse. There was no place for us to lie down and sleep, nor could our animals lie down; the water had given out, and the prospect was indeed gloomy — the canyon had been leading us directly north. All agreed that the animals were too jaded and worn to go back.

Then we called the men: "What did they tell you at Fort Hall about the northern region?"

They repeated, "You must not go too far north; if you do you will get into difficult canyon that lead towards the Columbia River, where you may become bewildered and wander about and perish."

This canyon was going nearly north; in fact it seemed a little east of north. We sent some men to see if they could reach the top of the mountain by scaling the precipice somewhere and get a view, and they came back about ten or eleven o'clock, saying the country looked better three or four miles farther ahead.

So we were encouraged. Even the animals seemed to take courage, and we got along much better than had been thought possible, and by one o'clock that day came out on what is now known as the Humboldt River. It was not until four years later (1845) that General Frémont first saw this river and named it Humboldt.

Our course was first westward and then southward, following this river for many days, till we came to its Sink, near which we saw a solitary horse, an indication that trappers had sometime been in that vicinity. We tried to catch him but failed; he had been there long enough to become very wild.

We saw many Indians on the Humboldt, especially towards the Sink. There were many tule marshes. The tule is a rush, large, but here not very tall. It was generally completely covered with honeydew, and this in turn was wholly covered with a pediculous-looking insect which fed upon it. The Indians gathered quantities of the honey and pressed it into balls about the size of one's fist, having the appearance of wet bran. At first we greatly relished this Indian food, but when we saw what it was made of — that the insects pressed into the mass were the main ingredient—we lost our appetites and bought no more of it.

From the time we left our wagons many had to walk, and more and more as we advanced. Going down the Humboldt at least half were on foot. Provisions had given out;

except a little coarse green grass among the willows along the river the country was dry, bare, and desolate; we saw no game except antelope, and they were scarce and hard to kill; and walking was very fatiguing.

Tobacco lovers would surrender their animals for anyone to ride who would furnish them with an ounce or two to chew during the day. One day one of these devotees lost his tobacco and went back for it, but failed to find it. An Indian in a friendly manner overtook us, bringing the piece of tobacco, which he had found on our trail or at our latest camp, and surrendered it. The owner, instead of being thankful, accused the Indian of having stolen it—an impossibility, as we had seen no Indians or Indian signs for some days. Perhaps the Indian did not know what it was, else he might have kept it for smoking. But I think otherwise, for, patting his breast, he said, "Shoshone, Shoshone," which was the Indian way of showing he was friendly. The Shoshones were known as always friendly to the whites, and it is not difficult to see how other and distant tribes might claim to be Shoshones as a passport to favor.

9

On the Humboldt we had a further division of our ranks. In going down the river we went sometimes on one side and sometimes on the other, but mostly on the north side, till we were nearing what are now known as the Humboldt Mountains. We were getting tired, and some were in favor of leaving the oxen, of which we then had only about seven or eight, and rushing on into California. They said there was plenty of beef in California. But some of us said: "No; our oxen are now our only supply of food. We are doing well, making eighteen or twenty miles a day."

One morning when it was my turn at driving the oxen, the captain traveled so fast that I could not keep up, and was left behind. When night came I had to leave the trail and go over a rocky declivity for a mile and a half into a gloomy, damp bottom, and unpack the oxen and turn them out to eat, sleeping myself without blankets. I got up the next morning, hunted the oxen out of the willow thicket, and repacked them. Not having had supper or breakfast, and having to travel nine miles before I overtook the party, perhaps I was not in the best humor.

They were waiting, and for the very good reason that they could have nothing to eat till I came up with the oxen and one could be killed. I felt badly treated, and let the captain know it plainly; but, much to my surprise, he made no reply, and none of his men said a word. We killed an ox, ate our breakfast, and got ready to start about one or two o'clock in the afternoon. When nearly ready to go, the captain and one or two of his mess came to us and said: "Boys, our animals are better than yours, and we always get out of meat before any of the rest of you. Let us have the most of the meat this time, and we will pay you back the next ox we kill."

We gladly let them have all they wished. But as soon as they had taken it, and were mounted ready to start, the captain in a loud voice exclaimed: "Now we have been found fault with long enough, and we are going to California. If you can keep up with us, all right; if you cannot, you may go to ——"; and away they started, the captain and eight men.

One of the men would not go with the captain; he said, "The captain is wrong, and I will stay with you, boys."

In a short time they were out of sight. We followed their trail for two or three days, but after they had crossed over to the south side of the Humboldt and turned south we came into a sandy waste when the wind had entirely obliterated their tracks. We were then thrown entirely upon our own resources. It was our desire to make as great speed as possible west-ward, deviating only when obstacles inter-posed, and in such case bearing south instead of north, so as to be found in a lower latitude in the event that winter should overtake us in the mountains. But, diverted by following our fugitive captain and party across the Hum-boldt, we thereby missed the luxuriant Truc-kee meadows lying but a short distance to the west, a resting-place well and favorably known to later emigrants.

So, perforce, we followed down to the Sink of the Humboldt and were obliged to drink its water, which in the fall of the year becomes stagnant and of the color of lye, and not fit to drink or use unless boiled. Here we camped.

Leaving the Sink of the Humboldt, we crossed a considerable stream which must have been Carson River, and came to an-other stream which must have been Walker River, and followed it up to where it came out of the mountains, which proved to be the Sierra Nevada. We did not know the name of the mountains. Neither had these rivers then been named; nor had they been seen by Kit Carson or Joe Walker, for whom they were named, nor were they seen until 1845 by Fré-mont, who named them.

We were now camped on Walker River, at

the very eastern base of the Sierra Nevada, and had only two oxen left. We sent men ahead to see if it would be possible to scale the mountains, while we killed the better of the two oxen and dried the meat in preparation for the ascent. The men returned towards evening and reported that they thought it would be possible to ascend the mountains, though very difficult. We had eaten our supper, and were ready for the climb in the morning. Looking back on the plains we saw something coming, which we decided to be Indians. They traveled very slowly, and it was difficult to understand their movements. To make a long story short, it was the eight men that had left us nine days before. They had gone farther south than we and had come to a lake, probably Carson Lake, and there had found Indians who supplied them plentifully with fish and pine nuts. Fish caught in such water are not fit to eat at any time, much less in the fall of the year. The men had all eaten heartily of fish and pine nuts, and had got something akin to cholera morbus.

We were glad to see them although they had deserted us. We ran out to meet them and shook hands, and put our frying-pans on and gave them the best supper we could. Captain Bartleson, who when we started from Missouri was a portly man, was reduced to half his former girth. He said: "Boys, if I ever get back to Missouri I will never leave that country. I would gladly eat out of the troughs with my dogs." He seemed to be heartily sick of his late experience, but that did not prevent him from leaving us twice after that.

10

We were now in what is at presentNevada, and probably within forty miles of the present boundary of California. We ascended the mountains on the north side of Walker River to the summit, and then struck a stream running west which proved to be the extreme source of the Stanislaus River. We followed it down for several days and finally came to where a branch ran into it, each forming a canyon.The main river flowed in a precipitous gorge in places apparently a mile deep, and the gorge that came into it was but little less formidable. At night we found ourselves on the extreme point of the promontory between the two, very tired, and with neither grass nor water. We had to stay there that night.

Early the next morning two men went down to see if it would be possible to get through down the smaller canyon. I was one of them, Jimmy John the other. Benjamin

Kelsey, who had shown himself expert in finding the way, was now, without any election, still recognized as leader, as he had been during the absence of Bartleson.

A party also went back to see how far we should have to go around before we could pass over the tributary canyon. The understanding was, that when we went down the canyon if it was practicable to get through we were to fire a gun so that all could follow; but if not, we were not to fire, even if we saw game.

When Jimmy and I got down about three-quarters of a mile I came to the conclusion that it was impossible to get through, and said to him, "Jimmy, we might as well go back; we can't go here."

"Yes, we can," said he; and insisting that we could, he pulled out a pistol and fired. It was an old dragoon pistol, and reverberated like a cannon.

I hurried back to tell the company not to come down, but before I reached them the captain and his party had started. I explained, and warned them that they could not get down; but they went on as far as they could go, and then were obliged to stay all day and night to rest the animals, and had to go about among the rocks and pick a little grass for them, and go down to the stream through a terrible place in the canyon to bring water up in cups and camp-kettles, and some of the men in their boots, to pour down the animals' throats in order to keep them from perishing. Finally, four of them pulling and four of them pushing a mule, they managed to get them up one by one, and then carried all the things up again on their backs—not an easy job for exhausted men.

In some way, nobody knows how, Jimmy got through that canyon and into the Sacramento Valley. He had a horse with him—an Indian horse that was bought in the Rocky Mountains, and which could come as near climbing a tree as any horse I ever knew. Jimmy was a character. Of all men I have ever known I think he was the most fearless; he had the bravery of a bulldog. He was not seen for two months—until he was found at Sutter's, afterwards known as Sutter's Fort, now Sacramento City.

We went on, traveling west as near as we could. When we killed our last ox we shot and ate crows or anything we could kill, and one man shot a wild-cat. We could eat anything.

One day in the morning I went ahead, on foot of course, to see if I could kill something, it being understood that the company would keep on as near west as possible and find a practicable road. I followed an Indian trail down into the canyon, meeting many Indians on the way up. They did not molest me, but I did not quite like their looks. I went about ten miles down the canyon, and then began to think it time to strike north to intersect the trail of the company going west.

A most difficult time I had scaling the precipice. Once I threw my gun up ahead of me, being unable to hold it and climb, and then was in despair lest I could not get up where it was, but finally I did barely manage to do so, and made my way north. As the darkness came on I was obliged to look down and feel with my feet lest I should pass over the trail of the party without seeing it.

Just at dark I came to an enormous fallen tree and tried to go around the top, but the place was too brushy, so I went around the butt, which seemed to me to be about twenty or twenty-five feet above my head. This I suppose to have been one of the fallen trees in the Calaveras Grove of *Sequoia gigantea* or mammoth trees, as I have since been there, and to my own satisfaction identified the lay of the land and the tree. Hence I concluded that I must have been the first white man who ever saw the *Sequoia gigantea,* of which I told

Frémont when he came to California in 1844.

Of course sleep was impossible, for I had neither blanket nor coat, and burned or froze alternately as I turned from one side to the other before the small fire which I had built, until morning, when I started eastward to intersect the trail, thinking the company had turned north. But I traveled until noon and found no trail; then striking south, I came to the camp which I had left the previous morning. The party had gone, but not where they had said they would go; for they had taken the same trail I had followed, into the canyon, and had gone up the south side, which they had found so steep that many of the poor animals could not climb it and had to be left.

When I arrived the Indians were there cutting the horses to pieces and carrying off the meat. My situation, alone among strange Indians killing our poor horses, was by no means comfortable. Afterward we found that these Indians were always at war with the Californians. They were known as the Horse Thief Indians, and lived chiefly on horse flesh; they had been in the habit of raiding the ranches even to the very coast, driving away horses by the hundreds into the mountains to eat. That night after dark I overtook the party in camp.

A day or two later we came to a place where there was a great quantity of horse bones, and we did not know what it meant; we thought that an army must have perished there. They were of course horses that the Indians had driven in there and slaughtered. A few nights later, fearing depredations, we concluded to stand guard—all but one man, who would not. So we let his two horses roam where they pleased. In the morning they could not be found. A few miles away we came to a village; the Indians had fled, but we found the horses killed and some of the meat roasting on a fire.

11

We were now on the edge of the San Joaquin Valley, but we did not even know that we were in California. We could see a range of mountains lying to the west,—the Coast Range,—but we could see no valley. The evening of the day we started down into the valley we were very tired, and when night came our party was strung along for three or four miles, and every man slept right where darkness overtook him. He would take off his saddle for a pillow and turn his horse or mule loose, if he had one. His animal would be too poor to walk away, and in the morning he would find him, usually within fifty feet. The jaded horses nearly perished with hunger and fatigue.

When we overtook the foremost of the party the next morning we found they had come to a pond of water, and one of them had killed a fat coyote; when I came up it was all eaten except the lights and the windpipe, on which I made my breakfast.

From that camp we saw timber to the north of us, evidently bordering a stream running west. It turned out to be the stream that we had followed down in the mountains—the Stanislaus River. As soon as we came in sight of the bottom land of the stream and saw an abundance of antelopes and sandhill cranes. We killed two of each the first evening. Wild grapes also abounded. The next day we killed thirteen deer and antelopes, jerked the meat and got ready to go on, all except the captain's mess of seven or eight, who decided to stay there and lay in meat enough to last them into California!

We were really almost down to tidewater, but did not know it. Some thought it was five hundred miles yet to California. But all thought we had to cross at least that range of mountains in sight to the west before entering the promised land, and how many more beyond no one could tell. Nearly all thought it best to press on lest the snows might overtake us in the mountains before us, as they had already nearly done on the mountains behind us (the Sierra Nevada).

It was now about the first of November.

Our party set forth bearing northwest, aiming for a seeming gap north of a high mountain in the chain to the west of us. That mountain we found to be Mount Diablo. At night the Indians attacked the captain's camp and stole all their animals, which were the best in the company, and the next day the men had to overtake us with just what they could carry in their hands.

The next day, judging by the timber we saw, we concluded there was a river to the west. So two men went ahead to see if they could find a trail or a crossing. The timber seen proved to be along what is now known as the San Joaquin River.

We sent two men on ahead to spy out the country. At night one of them returned, saying they had come across an Indian on horseback without a saddle who wore a cloth jacket but no other clothing. From what they could understand the Indian knew Dr. Marsh and had offered to guide them to his place. He plainly said "Marsh," and of course we supposed it was the Dr. Marsh before referred to who had written the letter to a friend in Jackson County, Missouri, and so it proved. One man went with the Indian to Marsh's ranch and the other came back to tell us what he had done, with the suggestion that we should go on and cross the river (San Joaquin) at the place to which the trail was leading.

In that way we found ourselves two days later at Dr. Marsh's ranch, and there we learned that we were really in California and our journey at an end. After six months we had now arrived at the first settlement in California, November 4, 1841.

The account of our reception, and of my own experiences in California in the pastoral period before the gold discovery, I must reserve for another paper.

When Frederic Remington drew this picture he called it "A Recruit from Civilization."

Near the junction of the forks of the Platte.

Fort Laramie, famous stopping-place on the Oregon Trail.

One of the most popular engravings of emigrants crossing the plains, from a drawing by F. O. C. Darley, a noted and versatile illustrator much earlier than Remington. Another western picture by him, "Emigrants Attacked by Indians on the Prairie" was ordered by Prince Napoleon of France.

"The Ox-driver," from a painting by Harvey T. Dunn. Said the poet Sam Simpson, "And the men, with set lips, stalk on by their teams as the endless white road goes winding and winding."

The Elijah White Train on the way to Oregon in 1842.

The evening camp—bacon, mountain biscuit, coffee.

From The Dalles some of the White party followed the trail on the north side of the Columbia

2

FIRST EMIGRANT TRAIN
TO OREGON

Elm Grove to Oregon City
May 16 to October 5, 1842

Five members of Elijah White's party of 1842 left first-hand accounts of the trip, one of them in a diary, two in records a few years afterwards, and two in recollections after they were old men.

Medorem Crawford's Journal: An Account of His Trip Across the Plains with the Oregon Pioneers of 1842 *was published in a pamphlet of 26 pages in 1897 by the University of Oregon.*

Twenty-three-year-old Loren L. Hastings, opposed

to White and replacing him as captain of the train, return to Cincinnati with his manuscript but no money for printing it. He secured funds by joining up with a Methodist preacher for a lecture tour, not on Oregon and California but on temperance. His Emigrants Guide to Oregon and California, 152 pages, Cincinnati, 1845, was reprinted in facsimile by the Princeton University Press in 1932. Medorem Crawford marked his copy of the book with such expressions as "Reckless exageration", "Absolutely false", "Bosh", "Silly lies", "Phenomenal Lying", "Nonsense".

White's own version of the journey was given in Ten Years in Oregon, 399 pages, compiled by Miss A. J. Allen, Ithaca, New York, 1848.

F. X. Matthieu, who joined the train at Fort Laramie, dictated his recollections of the trip to Samuel A. Clarke in the Oregonian 1886 and to H. L. Lyman in the Oregon Historical Quarterly 1900. An interview with A. L. Lovejoy by Henry R. Reed was printed as "Lovejoy's Pioneer Narrative" in the Oregon Historical Quarterly 1930.

A juvenile novel on this emigration, Dog of the Pioneer Trail by Delia Morris Stephenson, was published by Binfords & Mort in 1937.

The best historical accounts of the journey are by Hubert Howe Bancroft in History of Oregon 1886 and by Samuel A. Clarke in Pioneer Days of Oregon History 1905.

In this volume the basic narrative is Bancroft's with numerous annotations from the other sources.

Elijah White Party

By HUBERT HOWE BANCROFT

and Others

1

[DR. ELIJAH WHITE was familiar with the far end of the Oregon Trail, but not with the trail itself. He had spent about three years as physician at the Methodist Mission, until he quarreled with Jason Lee and returned to the States in disgust. He had gone to and come back from Oregon by ship, not overland by the long, long route of the trappers. The vast Oregon Country was under so-called joint occupation, really pretty much in the hands of the British through the Hudson's Bay Company. The few American settlers felt like orphans in the wilderness. They wanted the United States to send somebody out to give them and the Indians the protection of American laws.]

After considerable discussion the government decided that as the United States made pretensions to the territory lying between the Rocky Mountains and the Pacific Ocean, they might venture to send a sub-Indian agent into the country to look after the intercourse between the natives and the citizens of the United States.

White was commissioned sub-Indian agent, with a salary of seven hundred and fifty dollars. He was also verbally given permission to draw upon government funds for the payment of necessary expenses in the discharge of his duties. His instructions were to lose no time in returning to Oregon, but to proceed at once overland, using by the way every reasonable effort to induce immigrants to accompany him.

On reaching home, the doctor arranged his affairs and proceeded westward, making known his desire to raise a company for Oregon wherever he went, by advertising in the papers, and occasionally lecturing to interested audiences. White gives the following glimpse of his emigration efforts: "Last night all the other appointments were taken up to hear me lecture on Oregon, and as the weather was fine and traveling good, the noble church was filled, the pulpit lined with ministers of all denominations, and I talked an hour and a half with all my might."

At St. Louis everything relating to Oregon was heard with attention. The farther he progressed in the direction of Independence, the former recruiting rendezvous of the now disbanded fur companies, the greater was the interest evinced. From the latter place White made excursions through the country, from which a large number of immigrants were gained, while others appeared at Elm Grove, the appointed rendezvous twenty miles southwest of Independence.

2

By the 14th of May, 1842, one hundred and twelve persons were assembled, fifty-two being men over eighteen years of age.

[Most prominent were White, aged thirty-five, first captain of the train, and Lansford W. Hastings, captain the rest of the time, with little use for each other and splitting the company into factions. Medorem Crawford, who became a teacher, ferryman, legislator, Lincoln appointee; and F. X. Matthieu, joining the train at Fort Laramie, a former clerk of the American Fur Company. These four left accounts of the emigration. A. L. Lovejoy, one of the founders of Portland; Sidney Walter Moss who surveyed Oregon City for Dr. John McLoughlin, ran a hotel there, and claimed he was author of the first Oregon novel, *The Prairie Flower;* Stephen H. L. Meek, brother of the famous Joe Meek and later guide on Meek's Horrible Cut-Off; the two McKay boys, grandsons of Mrs. John McLoughlin; three Smiths, one with comely daughters whom the Sioux braves very much wanted to buy. From Fort Laramie to Fort Hall, the guide at a fee of $500 was the celebrated Thomas Fitzpatrick, who had guided the Bidwell party the year before.]

White's company was not so favorably circumstanced as those which had traveled under the protection of the American Fur Company. He says that his heart sank when he began to realize what he had undertaken; and that it was not made more buoyant when Sublette assured him that there would be much difficulty in organizing and governing such a large party, and in conducting it successfully such a distance through a wilderness infested with hostile Indian tribes. But Sublette gave valuable advice with regard to outfit and regulations.

The resolutions adopted were substantially as follows: That every male over 18 years of age should be provided with one mule or horse, or wagon conveyance. Should have one gun, 3 pounds of powder, 12 pounds of lead, 1,000 caps, or suitable flints; 50 pounds of flour or meal, 30 pounds of bacon, and a suitable proportion of provisions for women and children. That White should show his official appointment. That they elect a captain for one month. That there be elected a scientific corps of three persons to keep a record of everything concerning the road and journey that might be useful to the government or future emigrants. Elected were a pilot and a secretary; appointed were a blacksmith, master wagon-maker, and master road and bridge builder. That a code of laws be drafted and submitted to the company, and that they be enforced by reprimand, fines, and final banishment. That there be no profane swearing, obscene conversation, or immoral conduct allowed in the company, on pain of expulsion. That the names of every man, woman, and child be registered by the secretary.

The train of eighteen large Pennsylvania wagons, with a long procession of horses, pack-mules, and cattle, set out on the 16th, White having been elected to the command for one month from the time of starting.

As they left their beautiful encampment, it was a noble sight [as reported by Miss A. J. Allen in *Ten Years in Oregon*]. The eighteen wagons with their snow white coverings, winding down the long hill, followed by the immense train of horses, mules, and cattle of all kinds, their drivers walking by their side, merrily singing, or whistling, to beguile their way. As Dr. White stood on an elevation, he cast his eyes forward towards the wastes and wilds of the savage world they were to traverse, and back to his own loved, pleasant land, and it need not be inquired whether his reflections were of a very joyous nature.

According to regulations, camp was made at four o'clock every afternoon when wood and water were convenient. After the wagons had been drawn up so as to form a circular enclosure, the animals were turned loose to feed till sunset, when they were brought in and tethered to stakes set about the camp.

Every family had its own fire and prepared meals in its own fashion. The evening was spent in visiting, singing, and whatever innocent amusement suggested itself. The women and children slept in the covered wagons, and the men under tents on the ground.

A guard was stationed at night. At dawn, at a given signal, everyone arose and went about his duties, the cattle being collected while breakfast was being prepared. When all was ready, the wagon which had taken the lead the previous day was sent to the rear, so that each in rotation should come to the front.

In this manner all progressed amicably until the company had turned off from the Santa Fe Trail in a northwesterly direction to the crossing of the Kansas River.

3

At this point White startled the company by officially recommending that all the dogs in camp be forthwith killed lest they should go mad upon the arid plains which they were now approaching. King Herod's edict anent the slaughter of the innocents could scarcely have called forth a louder wail of lamentation from the mothers of Judea than was evoked from the women and children of White's party by this proposed immolation of their canine pets and companions. Many of the men, too, protested loudly against the sacrifice. Although when it came to a vote most of them yielded to their leader's wish, yet the measure was so unpopular that it contributed largely to the election of L. W. Hastings as captain at the end of the first month.

[For a fuller flavor of this dog episode, which has become rather celebrated in emigrant story, there are added here four vivid commentaries—from the book on White called *Ten Years in Oregon;* a diary entry by Medorem Crawford, a member of the company; a paragraph by W. J. Ghent in *The Road to Oregon;* and a fictionized excerpt from *Dog of the Pioneer Trail* by Delia Morris Stephenson]:

They passed on to the southwest, leaving the Santa Fe Trail to the left, nothing out of the common routine occurring till they reached what they afterwards designated as the dog encampment.

Here, by a two-thirds vote, it was determined to

kill all the dogs of the company, having been informed that, in crossing the mountains and their
vicinity, these animals were apt to become rabid, as
timber was scarce, and consequently water which
they so much required in the heats of summer on
the scorching plains. The arrangement did not at all
accord with the feelings of the ladies, and caused the
first serious disturbance since leaving the States.
While the destruction was going on, the poor crea-
tures would run to their mistresses for protection,
crying most piteously. Even the men, while engaged
in their task, found their hearts were not sufficiently
steeled to permit its performance without feelings of
sorrow and regret. However, the recollection of a
freshly related account of the mad wolf which had
bitten eleven of two encampments, strengthened
their fortitude. The death of the dogs was preferred
to those of their herds, and perhaps members of their
families, and they went resolutely about the work,
amid the cries and screams of the women and children, as well as of the victims.

[May 18]. A volent rain this morning. much excitement in camp about Dogs: 22 dogs shot. stopped
raining at 9 o'c.

The Emigration of 1842 really begins the epic of
the settlement of Oregon. . . . It was a party of
divergent wills, and it had a stormy time. There was
evidently too many dogs in the party, and at a meeting it was resolved to kill all of them. They would
all go mad on the plains, it was argued, and even if
they didn't they would be sure, by their barking and
growling, to acquaint any prowling Indians with the
fact that here was a party to be plundered. The
counter argument that their barking would also
apprise the emigrants of the presence of Indians did

not, apparently, carry sufficient weight, and a motion was passed that all the dogs be shot. Medorem Crawford, in his journal, and Miss A. J. Allen, the author of the book of White's travels, [the two authorities just quoted], say that the dogs—a total of twenty-two —were killed. Hastings, however, [later captain of the company] says that the motion produced a great deal of ill-feeling; that after a few were killed one owner after another declared that any man attempting to shoot his dog would himself be shot, and that as a consequence the execution stopped then and there.

It was a clear night on the plains. Certain dogs, seeming to remember that they were homesick, howled dismally at the moon. Others, seeing rabbits playing about in the moonlight, quite naturally joined in the game, making plenty of noise about it. Abby wished she could join them. It was hot and stuffy in the wagon. . . A coyote yapped insultingly from beyond a little draw. The dogs gave back full-throated and derisive answers.

Then everything quieted down for a while. Abner and Abby were both dropping off to sleep when the most terrific barking began. It was as if every dog were simply tearing his throat out. . .

It was not until morning that the loss of the cows was discovered. Then Dr. White laid it all on the dogs with their romping in the moonlight—the dogs who had done their level best to warn the party!

"You will recall," boomed Dr. White, "that I have already referred to the dogs of this party as a menace. My statement is borne out by the happenings of last night and I therefore offer a resolution to the effect that we proceed now, today, to the immediate and indiscriminate slaughter of all dogs within our midst."

Hastings was furious. "Nobody's killing my dog!"

A heated argument followed. The question was put to the vote and passed by a very small majority.

Dr. White rose to his feet. "Is there anything further to come before us? If not, we shall proceed to the immediate execution of this order."

The children looked at each other aghast. Then he meant to do it! What a terrible, cruel man!

Warning Shep not to bark, the three made one long streak back to camp.

"We'll just tell mother," gasped Abby, "and she'll just see if he kills our Shep."

"Yes," panted Abner, "and I'll get that Mr. Hastings to help us. I bet he'll tell that mean old Dr. White a thing or two!"

4

At this camp Columbia Lancaster lost a child, and as the mother was ill, the disheartened parents turned back.

The Kansas River, the South Platte, and other deep fords were made by placing boards across the tops of the wagon-boxes, on which the load was fastened, while above were perched the women and children. Soon after passing the South Fork, the company was overtaken by Stephen H. L. Meek, brother of Joe Meek, and one Bishop traveling for his health.

After Hastings was elected to succeed White, harmony no longer prevailed. The determination of the new commander to "govern and not be governed" divided the party into two factions, who marched in separate columns till Fort Laramie was reached on the 23rd of June. Here they spent a week in refitting. During that time Mr. Bissonette, in charge of the post, managed to bring about a reunion by urging that the company would need its full strength while passing through the hostile tribes between Laramie and Fort Hall.

As the emigrants were told that it would be impossible for them to take their oxen and wagons through to Oregon, many sold or exchanged them for horses, the advantage being generally on the side of the fort people. They also laid in a fresh stock of provisions for which they had to pay at the rate of a dollar a pint for flour, and a dollar a pound for coffee and sugar. "They disposed of their wagons and cattle at the fort," said Fremont, "selling them at the prices they had paid in the States, and taking in exchange coffee and sugar at one dollar a pound, and miserable, worn-out horses which died before they reached the mountains. Mr. Boudeau informed me that he had purchased 30 and the lower fort 80 head of fine cattle, some of them of the Durham breed."

Before leaving Laramie the company was

joined by F. X. Matthieu and half a dozen Canadians, who had been in the service of the fur company east of the Rocky Mountains, and were now going to settle in Oregon. They had few supplies but depended on game for subsistence.

[They went supperless the first night out, as Matthieu recalled in his reminiscences fifty-eight years later. "They could not but look on with a little envy and self-commiseration at the various campfires where the immigrants were despatching fried bacon and mountain biscuit and drinking coffee." Matthieu also recalled what four of the leading men of the party were like—White "a sleek looking gentleman; a quick talker"; sandy complexioned Amos L. Lovejoy "more quick tempered than any man I ever knew"; Captain Hastings of heavy build and swarthy complexion; Captain Fitzpatrick, the guide, a tall, spare, gray-haired Irishman of gentlemanly bearing, at home anywhere in the mountains or on the prairies, but very taciturn.]

They had hardly proceeded a mile from Fort Laramie before they met Bridger and Fitzpatrick, the former being on his way to the States with a large quantity of furs, and accompanied through the hostile country by the latter. As Bridger no longer required his services, Fitzpatrick was induced by White to guide the company to Fort Hall at the expense of the government.

5

The new guide soon had an opportunity to show his skill in dealing with the natives. While at Independence Rock, where some of the party were ambitious to inscribe their names, Hastings and Lovejoy, who had fallen behind, were cut off by a party of Sioux. They narrowly escaped to camp after several hours of detention, the savages following and being met by Fitzpatrick, who succeeded in arranging matters.

We were treated with the utmost rudeness [said Hastings of their situation after they climbed down from carving their names to find themselves captured]. Our guns and pistols were taken from us, when we were compelled to sit upon the ground, surrounded by a numerous guard who performed its *whole duty,* not permitting us to change our positions in any manner, either to avoid danger or acquire comfort. From the time we were taken, every additional party that arrived invariably offered some indignity to our persons, either by striking or attempting to strike us with their bows, arrows, or the rammers of their guns. The chief, however, protected me from this insult, for which purpose he constantly stood or sat by me; yet he appeared unable or unwilling to protect my companion, who was repeatedly stricken with much violence.

A great band of Sioux developed out of the prairie [said Matthieu], galloping in wild fashion upon their ponies or in large part running on foot . . . in full war dress and paint. Lovejoy and Hastings were among them, being held as captives and looking very much crestfallen. They had delayed, as it seems, in boyish spirit, to inscribe their names among others on the face of Independence Rock; and having just completed their task, had turned to go only to find themselves in the embrace of some very large Indians. [They wanted ammunition, not to fight the whites but other Indians; when this was given to them they surrendered Hastings and Lovejoy.]

The Sweetwater was reached on the 13th of July, and here one of the company, a young man named Bailey, was accidentally shot by another of the party.

He, poor fellow, [said White], died in thirty minutes. He was a useful man, and it gave a dreadful shock to us all. The next day at eight o'clock, as there was no clergyman, I was called upon to deliver a funeral discourse, near Independence Rock, in the midst of the mountains. While I talked to all the company, who went on foot a mile to the grave, a general weeping prevailed among us. When, in the course of my brief solemn lecture, I said, "Let us pray," to my astonishment nearly every man, woman, and child dropped upon their knees to implore the divine blessing and protection. It was the most solemn funeral by far that any of us ever attended or probably ever will.

[Wrote Crawford in his diary]: July 14. Buried Baily near Independence Rock ½ mile from camp. My feelings on this occasion can hardly be described. A young man . . . wrapped in a Buffalo Robe & buried in this dismal Prairie.

At this place all remained for several days to hunt buffalo and dry the meat. The Sioux, who infested the country in considerable numbers, caused the hunters great annoyance, frequently robbing them of both horses and game, though they were kept at a safe distance from camp. The last that was seen of them was on a tributary of the Sweetwater, where the principal chiefs were invited to camp and conciliated with presents.

[Matthieu, through two historians, said of this period of Indian embarrassment: "About five or six thousand of the Blackfoot Sioux, under a great war chief, appeared. By this immense multitude the train was compelled to halt and to be inspected by band after band of the curious savages. They were especially curious to look at the women of the train." The braves came cautiously to Smith's tent, pulled the flaps apart, and gazed in silent admiration upon his wife and daughters. Smith appealed to Matthieu to get rid of them. "All but one young fellow withdrew. He said he wanted to have a talk with the old chief (Smith) and inquired every moment what Smith said about him. At last Matthieu explained to Smith that the Sioux warrior offered twenty horses for his choice of his girls. Smith exclaimed, 'The brute!' Matthieu then explained to the savage that it was not the custom among whites to sell their women. The Sioux was ready for him then, for he remarked that 'he knew that the white men bought Indians girls, and why not have the rule work both ways?' He gave up the trade and went away reluctantly."]

As soon as they were clear of the enemy, White and a dozen others who were well mounted pushed on before, taking Fitzpatrick with them. This left Hastings in charge of the heavier portion of the train, without a guide, and accordingly caused much dissatisfaction.

At Green River another division occurred. About half the original number of wagons was still retained; and now a part persisted in cutting up their wagons and making pack-saddles, and traveling henceforth with horses. Heavy rainstorms hindered both parties, who arrived at Fort Hall about the same time. Here the emigrants were kindly received by Grant, who sold them flour for half the price paid at Laramie, taking in payment the running-gear of the wagons, which all now agreed to dispense with.

Attempts have been made to show that the Hudson's Bay Company's officers did what they could to obstruct immigration from the States, and purposely exaggerate the difficulties in order to induce the emigrants to sell their oxen and wagons at a sacrifice. That such was not the case is proved by Grant's kindness to White's and other parties. He sold them provisions low, and so far from trying to get their wagons, he assured them that they could travel with them as far as Walla Walla without serious interruption. It was their own fault if they did not take his advice. [Matthieu didn't remember it that way. Grant was large and fine looking, "as big a man as John McLoughlin." He told the emigrants it was impossible for wagons to cross the Blue Mountains into Oregon. Matthieu, however, believed Grant said this because he thought it was true—representing what was generally understood as a fact.]

6

The company remained at Fort Hall about ten days, except White's party, who started a few days in advance. They lost a man, Adam Horn, the unfortunate cause of Bailey's death, at the crossing of Snake River below Salmon Falls. The doctor and his companions started with McDonald, a Hudson's Bay trader; but the pack-animals not being able to keep up with the fur company's cavalcade, the greater number of the party fell behind, while White and a few others proceeded with McDonald to Walla Walla. The route after leaving Fort Boise was through Burnt River Canyon and Grande Ronde Valley, and thence over the Blue Mountains, which they crossed in two days. From the foot of the mountains an Indian guided White to Whitman's mission.

Hastings' party avoided the crossing of the Snake River, proceeding along the south side of that stream as far as the lower crossing at Fort Boise, where they came into the trail of the advance party. They also turned aside to visit Waiilatpu, where they were warmly welcomed by Whitman about the middle of September. Here they halted several days to recruit, and were kept busy answering the eager questions of the isolated missionaries concerning affairs in the States.

Lovejoy, who was of Hastings' party, had been left behind to search for a lost companion. When he reached Walla Walla, Hastings had gone, so he remained at the mission, and in the following month was engaged to accompany Whitman to the States.

[Some experiences of the wagonless, horse-back journey on from Fort Hall to Fort Walla Walla are given in more detail in three entries of Crawford's diary]:

Sept 3d . . . arrived at Fort Boyzea at 9. Crossed over Snake River in a Canoe to the Fort. . . Fort B. is a new Establishment. It has been a short time in operation but is not yet completed. We saw but one white man who was French. . . At the Fort we tasted musk mellon but of a very indifferent quality. . . Left camp at 11 o'clock & traveled briskly over a sandy country. suffered considerable for water as the day was exceedingly hot. came to a creek about 6 o'clock & never was water to me more exceptable though of a very indifferent quality, passed down the Creek a short distance at the foot of a mountain & found boiling water running out of the ground. . . One of our company cooked a fish which he caught from the creek in about two minutes perfectly through. The water was so salt that the fish was sufficiently seasoned.

Sept. 14. We arrived at 3 o'clock [at Dr. Whitman's] and camped near his house. Dr. Whitman is a Missionary of the Presbyterian Order he has been in the country six years. He has a very comfortable house and is farming to a considerable extent. He has a Threshing Machine & a grinding mill all under one roof drived by water power. Many Indians around him. I was never more pleased to see a house or white people in my life, we were treated by Dr. and Mrs. Whitman with the utmost kindness. We got what provisions we wanted on very reasonable terms. . .

Sept. 16. Started at 8 o'clock kept down the Wala-

wala River and camped at 1 o'clock within 3 miles of the Fort. . . Visited the Fort saw Esqr Crocker, Doctor White had left before noon in the Companies Boat. . . I had an introduction to Mr. McKenly who is in charge at the fort. The Fort is rebuilding now having lately been burnt. It is situated on a miserable sandy barren place where the sand drifts with the wind like snow. . .

From Waiilatpu the emigrants proceeded without accident to the Willamette Valley, which they reached on the 5th of October, some by Daniel Lee's cattle trail from The Dalles, and others by the trail on the north of the Columbia, swimming their cattle to the south side when opposite the mouth of Sandy River.

White, who appears to have been anxious to reach the settlements as early as possible, arrived at Vancouver about the 20th of September. Considering the circumstances of his departure from Oregon, it was but natural that he should have some feeling of self-importance and exultation on returning as the first officer of the United States appointed in that country.

[White, with his predilection for laws, worked out what was called the White Code for the behavior of the Indians. It had eleven articles. Article 9 showed he had not yet got over his prejudice against dogs: "Those only may keep dogs who travel, or live among the game; if a dog killed a lamb, a calf or any domestic animal, the owner shall pay the damage and kill the dog."]

3

FIRST EMIGRANT TRAIN TO WASHINGTON

Council Bluffs to Puget Sound
May 10 to October 8, 1853

This account was prepared by Mrs. Lou Palmer from personal interviews with James Longmire a few years before he died. The old frontiersman still made early spring trips to the foot of Mt. Rainier to his place there called Longmire Springs—with Buck, his riding horse, which was "deaf as a post," and Snoqualmie, his packhorse, which had ascended to the highest elevation on Rainier ever reached by a horse and had made more trips across the high Cascades than any other horse.

The narrative is abridged from its printing by the Secretary of State of Washington in 1937 in Told by the Pioneers. *It had previously been published three times over a period of forty years—in the* Tacoma Ledger *for August 21, 1892, filling more than a page in the small type of that newspaper; in the* Oregon Pioneer Transactions *for 1904; in the* Washington Historical Quarterly *for January 1932.*

Of the road over and through the Cascades prepared by the Puget Sound settlers for the emigrants, said the pioneer historian Elwood Evans, "Through the mountains a trail had been blazed — nothing more. Over the huge logs, bridges had been constructed, passable for horses but obstructions really to wagons. Fallen trees, the growth of centuries, lay across the path. Abrupt, dangerous, and steep river crossings, just as nature had made them after her floods, had washed away the banks. To call it a road was an abuse of language; but over it and by it did those immigrants of 1853 travel in their journey to Puget Sound . . . with axe in hand hewed their way through a mountain gorge . . . over a road built as they marched."

Through Naches Pass

By James Longmire

1

I started from our home on Shawnee Prairie, Indiana, with my wife and four children on the 6th day of March, 1853. My youngest child was not able to work when we started, but spent his evenings while on the trip in learning, which he did by supporting himself by holding to the tongue of the wagon while in camp.

I got a neighbor to drive us to Attica where we took passage on the *U. S. Ariel* on the Wabash River as far south as Evansville. From Evansville we took the steamer *Sparrow Hawk* for St. Louis, thence by the *Polar Star* up the Mississippi and Missouri rivers to St. Joseph. Here I bought eight yoke of oxen and a large quantity of supplies, and traveled along the river to Kanesville, now Council Bluffs. I bought a carriage and a span of horses for $250 which my wife and children were to use as far as the road would permit.

I also got a sheet-iron stove, which, with cooking utensils, only weighed twenty-five pounds, but which proved a real luxury, as we were able to have warm biscuits for breakfast whenever we chose. I only paid $12 for the stove, but it proved invaluable to us.

When we decided the grass was sufficient to feed our cattle on the way, we made our final start for Puget Sound on the 10th day of May, 1853. Nothing occurred worthy of note until two days afterwards when we reached the Elkhorn River.

John Lane started with some fine stock, among them a thoroughbred mare of great beauty, which we would not allow to swim with the rest of our stock safely across the stream. With a rope around her neck held by Sargent, and myself on one side of the river, and with himself and E. A. Light on the other side, we towed her across, but alas—dead! We landed her according to Lane's instructions and tried to revive the beautiful creature, but failed. Poor Sargent had to bear the blame, unjustly, I think, and only escaped blows from Lane, whose rage knew no bounds, by my interference. But Lane left our party.

Two hundred miles further on we came to Rawhide Creek. Here we stopped to rest our thoroughly tired, foot-sore oxen, and do our washing, which was not done always on Monday, to the annoyance of our excellent housekeepers.

We had killed a few antelopes along the road, which furnished the camp with what we thought the best steak we had ever eaten, and were fired with the resolve to secure a still greater luxury [They killed a huge buffalo]. We secured our horses and began to strip our game of his smooth coat, selecting the hind-quarters for our share, judging these to be the choice of cuts, which we were to put in a bag which we had carried for this purpose.

In about 15 minutes after we began our work we were surprised—yes, perfectly horrified—to see about thirty big, hungry grey wolves coming rapidly toward us, attracted no doubt by the scent of blood from the dead buffalo. Nearer and nearer they came, till, hearing a noise, we looked in the direction of our horses and saw them in wildest fright to the north, in a directly opposite course from our camp. We hurriedly left our game to the wolves, most willingly, and went in pursuit of our rapidly fleeing horses.

We crossed the Rocky Mountains at South Pass, according to the instructions given in *Horn's Guide for Emigrants,* which we had carefully observed during our trip. All went smoothly until we crossed Bear Mountains, when, feeling some confidence in our own judgment, we had grown somewhat careless about consulting our handbook.

I had gone ahead to find a camp for noon, which I did on a pretty stream with abundance of grass for our horses and cattle. Soon after dinner we noticed some of our cattle began to lag, and seem tired, and others began to vomit. We realized with horror that our cattle had been poisoned. Bacon and grease were the only antidotes for poison that our stores contained. So we cut slices of bacon and forced it down the throats of the sick oxen, who after once tasting the bacon, ate it eagerly, thereby saving their lives, as those that did not eat died the next day. Had we consulted our guidebook before instead of after camping at that pretty spot, we would have been spared all this trouble, as it warned travelers of the poison existing there.

At Salmon Falls we crossed the Snake River for the first time. Hutchinson had a fine lot of horses and cattle which caused him much anxiety, as he feared they might drown while crossing the river. There were many Indians here of the Snake tribe. He tried to hire one of them to swim his stock, for which he offered money, without making the least impression on the stolid creature. Finally taking off his outside shirt, a calico garment, Hutchinson offered it to him, which, to our surprise, he took.

I tried to get an Indian to swim our cattle, but failed, Watt proposed to go with them if I would. Watt carried a long stick in one hand. With the other he held on to the tail of Old Lube, a great, rawboned ox who had done faithful service on our long and toilsome journey. I threw my stick away and went in a little below Watt, but found the current very strong, which drifted me downstream. Thinking I should be drowned, I shouted at Watt, "I'm gone." He, with great presence of mind, reached his stick to me, which I grasped and by this means bore up till I swam to Watt, who caught on to the tail of the nearest ox, thus giving me hold on Old Lube's tail—welcome hold, too, and one which carried me safely to shore.

At Grand Ronde a happy surprise awaited us. Nelson Sargent, whose father was in our party, had met John Lane, who had arrived in advance of us, with the welcome news that a party of workmen had started out from Olympia and Steilacoom to make a road for us through the Naches Pass over the Cascades, ours being the first party of emigrants to attempt a crossing of the Columbia north of The Dalles.

We left the emigrant trail at Umatilla and with 36 wagons struck out for Fort Walla Walla, a trading post fifty miles further on, kept by an agent of the Hudson's Bay Company, of whom we bought lumber — driftwood from the Columbia River—of which we made a flatboat on which to ferry our goods across the river, afterwards selling or trading the boat to the agent in payment for the lumber.

On the 8th of September, at 2 o'clock in the afternoon, our boat was finished, and the task of crossing commenced—not a pleasing one, but by working all night everything was safely landed by sunrise next morning, except our horses and cattle, and these we wanted the Indians to take across for us.

Nelson Sargent was the only man in the crowd that could speak Chinook, but not well enough to make a bargain with the Indians. So we got the agent to hire them to swim our stock, but before they would commence work they must be paid. We gave them $18 and they brought up twenty-five canoes, forming them in line below the crossing. We drove our stock into the river and they swam to the opposite shore in safety. Next came the horses. When they were in the middle of the stream,

In July, 1834, Nathaniel Wyeth, American trader, built Fort Hall, naming it after his elder partner, Henry Hall. Wrote Wyeth: "Its bastions stand a terror to the sculking Indian and a beacon of safety to the fugitive hunter." By the time the White party to Oregon and the Naches Pass party to Puget Sound stopped here, Wyeth had been forced to sell Fort Hall to the Hudson's Bay Company.

Fort Walla Walla where the Naches Pass emigrants left the Oregon Trail, making a flatboat to carry themselves and their goods across the Columbia and hiring Indians with twenty-five canoes to swim their oxen and horses over.

Mt. Rainier, from an engraving in the Century Magazine for April 1885. Said James Longmire, "We followed Naches River for four days, crossing and recrossing sixty times. Then we left it and started for the summit of the Cascade Mountains, twenty-five miles north of Mt. Rainier."

Fort Nisqually, end of the Naches Pass Trail. "Mr. Tolmie, chief factor of the Hudson's Bay Company, paid a visit, asking us numerous questions about our long journey. He soon left but returned with a man driving an ox cart which was loaded with beef."

the treacherous Indians laid down their oars and made signs, which I understood to mean more money. Meanwhile our horses were drifting downstream where high bluffs were on either side, and it would be impossible for them to land. I took out my purse and offered them more money. They took up their oars and paddled across, landing our horses safely.

The chief of the Walla Wallas was Peu-Peu-Mox-Mox or Yellow Serpent, a very important person who rode, with the dignity of a king, a large American horse—a beautiful bay, with holsters on his saddle, and a pair of navy revolvers. He was a fine looking Indian, fully aware of his power as chief, well demonstrated when we were weighing some beef bought of him, cut in pieces from ten to twenty pounds, but it must be weighed. The chief went to Mr. Melville, the only man in our party who had scales, and taking them in his hand examined them carefully, although he could not tell one figure from another. Then he came to me and gave me the scales with a sign that I do the weighing. I weighed, Lane standing by with a book and pencil to tally. Every time a piece was weighed the chief would spring up, examine the scales closely, give a grunt which meant Yes, and sit down. He continued this until the last piece was weighed.

3

Our guide, who made a horse trade with Mr. Melville in which he considered himself cheated, grew indignant and deserted us. We were left in a strange country without a land-mark, a compass, or guide—nothing to help us. We traveled on, however, to the Yakima River, which we crossed.

Here we lost by death one of our party, Mr. McCullough, a relative of Mrs. Woolery. Until this sad event, Mrs. Woolery was the life, the sunshine of the party. Everyone loved Aunt Pop, as she was familiarly called, but this occurrence cast a shadow over her bright face, and made the remainder of the journey gloomy when we thought of the lonely grave on the banks of the Yakima.

Our next obstacle was a canyon at Wells Springs, which it seemed impossible to cross.

From the Yakima River we had been fol-lowed by a band of Indians, who had kept our wives and children in perfect terror, but they chatted and laughed as they rode along with us, the tyees or big men being dressed in buck-skin leggins handsomely embroidered, and breech-clouts made of cedar bark. The squaws were dressed much the same, all with painted faces. The squaws carried the papooses done up in proper Indian fashion and hung to the horns of the saddles, where they bobbed up and down in no easy fashion, especially when the ponies were in full gallop, as they were most of the time.

At Wells Springs we sent out men to find a better road, as we thought we were lost.

The Indians, knowing from this move that we were lost, got off their ponies, cleared a small piece of ground, and marked two roads, one leading to the northwest and the other to the northeast—making dots at intervals along each road, the latter having fewer dots than the former. One of them, motioning his hand in an upward and curving line, pointed with the other one to the dots, saying at each one, "Sleeps, sleeps," and at the end of the road, "Soldiers"—the only words we could understand and really all the English they could speak.

Lane said to me, "What shall we do?"

I replied, "Let us take the road with the fewest sleeps."

Which we did, going northeast for one or two days, when we discovered that we had taken the wrong road. [The one to Fort Colville, as they afterwards learned.] We had no compass, and we could have known little more if we had one. We saw before as a perpendicular bluff, which to us looked a thousand feet high, extending far away into the mountains and which we later learned was White Bluffs on the Columbia River.

Here we camped for the night, ordering the Indians to keep at a respectful distance, which they did, much to our surprise. However, we placed a double guard out, as we supposed they had led us into this trap in order to massacre our whole party. But I really believe now that their intentions were good, if they had only been able to make us understand them.

The next day we retraced our steps. Upon reaching Wells Springs, our Indians left us, much to our relief. We were further encouraged the same night by the return of Nelson Sargent, who, with others, had gone in advance to look out a good road—with the glad news that after crossing the canyon a good road lay before us; and still better news that they had struck a trail which the Steilacoom and Olympia Company had blazed for the coming emigrants.

On the 18th day of September, as well as I remember, we crossed the canyon, or rather traversed it, for about a mile of the roughest travel I ever experienced, and came out on a beautiful plain.

We traveled along Coal Creek for two days, when we came to Selah Valley on the upper Yakima, which we crossed, taking our course along Wenas Creek. Here we came to a garden kept by Indians, of whom we bought thirteen bushels of potatoes — a real feast, though boiled in their jackets.

Following Wenas Creek to its source, we crossed the Naches River, which we followed for four days, crossing and recrossing sixty-eight times. Then we left it and started for the summit of the Cascade Mountains, twenty-five miles north of Mount Rainier, which we reached in three days, finding fine grass and good water.

Here we stopped for a two-day rest, giving our tired oxen plenty of food, which they needed for the rest of the trip.

Three miles farther on we came to Summit Hill, where we spliced rope and prepared for the steep descent which we saw before us. One end of the rope was fastened to the axles of the wagons, the other end thrown around a tree and held by our men. Thus, one by one, the wagons were lowered gradually a distance of three hundred yards, when the ropes were loosened and the wagons drawn a quarter of a mile farther with locked wheels. Here we reached Greenwater River. All the wagons were lowered safely except the one belonging to Mr. Lane which was crushed to pieces by the breaking of one of the ropes, causing him and his family to make the rest of the trip on horseback.

[This account of Longmire's of letting the wagon down the mountain bluff omitted the most dramatic incident of all. Halted there by that drop-off in front of them, were the emigrants with their 36 wagons, 150 work oxen, 50 loose cattle, and 40 horses. A member of the company was George H. Himes, a barefooted boy of nine years and three months. The Oregon Historical Society files contain a long letter in his handwriting, dated January 23, 1905, and addressed to "My Dear Meeker", presumably Ezra Meeker. In the letter he gives Meeker his recollections fifty-two years back of that emigration of 1853 through Naches Pass, saying he had mislaid his notes on the trip and after searching high and low hadn't been able to turn them up. Possibly he found them later, for a typewritten manuscript adds a few details to what he had written to Meeker. By this time Himes was a famous man in the Pacific Northwest, a widely recognized authority on its history and in effect superintendent of the Oregon Historical Society. Here is the way he remembered how the wagons were got down that long steep place:

In due time the summit of the Cascades was reached. Here there was a small prairie—really it was an old burn that had not grown up to timber of any size. Now it was October and bitter cold to the youth with bare feet and fringed pants extending half way down from knees to feet. My father and the teams had left camp and gone across the little burn, where most of the company were assembled, apparently debating about the next movement to make. And no wonder, for as we neared we saw the cause of the delay. For a sheer thirty feet or more there was an almost perpendicular bluff, and for more than a thousand feet further down the mountain it was so steep that a team could not stand up.

It was at this point my mother exclaimed, after looking over the precipice, "Well, George, I guess we have got to the jumping-off place at last."

Heavy timber at all other points precluded the possibility of getting on by any other route. So the longest rope in the company was stretched down the cliff, leaving just enough to be used twice around a small tree which stood on the brink of the precipice, but it was found to be altogether too short.

Then James Biles said, "Kill one of the poorest of my steers and make his hide into a rope, and attach it to the one you have."

Three animals were slaughtered before a rope could be secured long enough to let the wagons down to a point where they would stand up. There one yoke of oxen were hitched to a wagon, and by locking the wheels and hitching on a small log with projecting limbs, it was taken down to a stream then known as Greenwater.

It took the best part of two days to make the descent. There were thirty-six wagons belonging to the company, but two of them, with a small quantity of provisions, were wrecked on this hill. The wagons could have been dispensed without much loss. Not so the provisions, scanty though they were, as the company came to be in sore straits for food before the White River Prairie was reached.

Now that this episode of rawhide made on the spot is preserved in the record, with its evidence of pioneer resourcefulness, the narrative is returned to Longmire.]

At the top of Summit Hill, my wife and Mrs. E. A. Light had gone ahead of the wagons with their children, taking the circuitous trail which brought them around to the wagon train, for which we were making the road as we went along. As they walked thus, my wife ahead, they were surprised to meet a white man. They had not seen one, except those of our party, since leaving Walla Walla, and little expected to find one in this almost inaccessible place, but were more than pleased by his rude welcome, "My God, women, where in the world did you come from?"

The two women shrank against the trees and shrubbery to give him room to pass them with his packhorses, the trail being barely wide enough for one person.

This man was Andy Burge, sent out from Fort Steilacoom with supplies for the road-makers who had already given up the job for want of food, which arrived too late for them but in time for us, as our stores were becoming alarmingly low. From these two lone women in the wilderness he learned of our whereabouts, and came at once to persuade us to return to where there was grass and water for our stock, telling us it was impossible for us to make our way over the country before us. Failing to convince us of this, he set to work to distribute his supplies among us, and returned to Fort Steilacoom, blazing trees as he went and leaving notes tacked up, giving what encouragement he could, and preparing us in a measure for what was before us.

For instance, he said, "The road is a shade better." A little farther on, "A shade worse." Then again, "A shade better." And so on till we were over the bad roads.

We crossed the Greenwater sixteen times and followed it until we came to White River, which we crossed six times. Then we left it for a dreary pull over Wind Mountain, which was covered with heavy fir and cedar trees but destitute of grass, with a few vine maples, on whose long leaves our poor oxen and horses had to live for seven long days, not having a blade of grass during that time.

I must not forget to mention that in these dark days—seven of them—we and our half-starved cattle worked the roads every day. We bridged large logs, which already lay on the ground, by cutting others and laying alongside them till we had a bridge wide enough for the oxen to draw our wagons across.

Then all, except John Lane, E. A. Light and myself, left their wagons on account of their failing oxen, which they drove before them to Boise Creek Prairie, where there was good grass. Lane, Light and I arrived first, the rest following soon afterwards with their cattle and horses. Four miles farther on we reached Porters Prairie. We again crossed White River, which made the seventh time, and pushed on to O'Connell Prairie, thence to Puyallup River.

We found the river low and filled with hump-back salmon. We armed ourselves with various weapons—clubs, axes, and whatever we could get—and all went fishing. Every man who could strike a blow got a fish and such a feast as we had not enjoyed since we had potatoes boiled in their jackets, only fish was far ahead of potatoes. John Meyers declared they were the best fish that he had ever eaten. Some of the party stayed up all night cooking and eating fish.

All relished them but my wife, who was indisposed, but she was fortunate enough in finding an Indian who had just killed a pheasant, which she bought—her first purchase on Puget Sound, and which caused merriment in our party, as the Indian was a perfect nude.

We moved on to Nisqually Plains and camped on Clover Creek, some three hundred yards away from the home of Mrs. Mahan. On the 9th of October, the day after we camped at Clover Creek, the men all went to Stilacoom Fort to see Puget Sound, leaving the women to keep camp. During their absence Mrs. Mahan took the ladies to her house, where she had prepared dinner which to these tired sisters, after their toilsome journey, was like a royal banquet. After months of camp life to sit once more at a table, presided over by a friend in this faraway land where we thought to meet only strangers, was truly an event never to be forgotten.

Before proceeding with my narrative, I will mention the fact of my arrival in this country with torn and ragged pants and coat, my cap tattered and torn, and with one boot on, the other foot covered with an improvised moccasin made from a piece of cowhide from one of the animals we had killed a few days previous.

In this garb I was to meet a party of well-dressed gentlemen from Olympia, who had heard of us from Andy Burge and who came out to welcome the first party of emigrants direct from the east over the Cascade Mountains north of The Dalles. My dress was a fair sample of that of the rest of the party. When together we felt pretty well, all being in the same fashion, but when brought face to face with well-dressed men I must confess I felt somewhat embarrassed. But our new friends were equal to the emergency. Our embarrassment was soon dispelled, while answering questions amid handshaking, hearty and genial.

On the 10th of October, Mr. Tolmie, chief factor of the Hudson's Bay Company at Fort Nisqually, paid a visit, asking us numerous questions about our long journey and arrival, and treating us in a very friendly manner, but soon left after bidding us a polite farewell. In about three hours he returned with a man driving an ox cart which was loaded with beef, just killed and dressed, which he presented to us, saying, "It is a present to you."

Leaving our families in camp, E. A. Light, John Lane and I started out to look for homes, after having received due notice from the Hudson's Bay Company not to settle on any land north of the Nisqually River. We crossed the river and went to Yelm Prairie. I bought a house from Martin Shelton but no land, as it was yet unsurveyed, and returned for my family.

When I returned to camp, Bill Harmon, who had a logging camp on Puget Sound, was waiting for me. He wanted my boys to work for him and offered them $85 per month. They declined until they saw me. I told them to go along, which they did, soon after getting an advance in salary to $100 per month.

We started to our new home, my wife and children in one wagon drawn by three yoke of oxen, which she drove. I went ahead with another wagon with four yoke of oxen.

Our carriage had long before been left on Burnt River, also the harness, which we saw afterwards on a pair of mules driven past us while on the emigrant trail.

Arriving at home, we found a large number

of Indians camped nearby. About thirty of them came the first night to examine things new to them, expressing surprise or satisfaction by grunts and guttural sounds which were Greek to us.

The following winter I took a donation claim.